Perseverance Is Key!

Unlocking the Internal Power of You

Regina M. Pontes

authorHOUSE®

AuthorHouse™
1663 Liberty Drive
Bloomington, IN 47403
www.authorhouse.com
Phone: 1 (800) 839-8640

Published by AuthorHouse 03/05/2018

ISBN: 978-1-5462-2727-4 (sc)
ISBN: 978-1-5462-2728-1 (e)

Library of Congress Control Number: 2018901422

DEDICATION

Words cannot adequately express my overwhelming love, gratitude, support and thanks to the following, but here it goes:

My Family: My unsung heroes --- my mother, Margaret, and father, the late Richard John Pontes; my big sisters, Patricia Haviland and Valerie Coll, and their husbands, David and Dennis, my late brother, Richard James Michael Pontes, my nieces and nephews, Michael, Kathryn, Daniel and Elizabeth and extended family. All of you rose to the challenges and were there for literally every step. A profound Thank You!

Dear Friends: All the members of Team Regina, especially Hunter and Nathan Barr; you two literally saved my life. Donna & Michael Dolan, my aunt Evelyn Finelli, Christine Viera, Greg Thompson, Karen and Tommy O'Connor, Jean Allen, Pam Aldred and Patti Hutchins also, the countless number of hospital staff, rehab facilities, doctors, therapists, and past and current caregivers. You know who you are, and for all of your help --- seeing me through so many illnesses --- all I can do is express a heartfelt Thank You! To Cynthia McGinty and Mike Nelson for all of your editing assistance. Your help was invaluable.

Finally: My PCP, and buddy, James E. Kolb, MD. What a crazy ride this 16-year odyssey has been so far. Love ya! Mean it! However, let's just plan to see each other for yearly check-ups and social events in the future only, shall we?!

FOREWORD

By James E. Kolb, MD

As we each travel along our life's journey, and if we are fortunate, we may meet someone who has the ability to inspire us in ways that may change our lives. It may be a humanitarian, it may be a famous artist, it may be a sports hero; but more than likely it is someone appearing to lead an ordinary life but who, in fact, is accomplishing extraordinary things. Regina's story is about the girl next-door who has accomplished extraordinary things.

I first met Regina in 1999. She had selected me to be her new internist. While taking her history, she shared the story of her twin brother who died by drowning under mysterious circumstances 3 years earlier. She shared how devastated she was about his death and how difficult it had been for her to complete her studies in California before returning home. Her family history was also notable for cancer. Despite being only 36 years old, we agreed that a baseline mammogram would be appropriate. Thankfully, it was normal. We discussed the importance of early and frequent cancer screening.

Two years passed before her next mammogram was performed. As she relates in her story, she was shocked to hear the news that at age 38 she was diagnosed with premenopausal breast cancer.

Imagine if you will that by age 38 this remarkable young woman had already sung at her twin brother's funeral and was now facing a lifetime of being a breast cancer survivor. With each passing day, she would face the prospect of recurrent cancer. Would that small lump in her breast be a new cancer? Would her next mammogram show a recurrent tumor? As she relates, complications of her original surgery led to the development of chronic lymphedema of her right upper extremity and recurrent cellulitis which at any time could be life-threatening.

Fast forward now through the next 14 years. She is forced to deal with a total abdominal hysterectomy with removal of both ovaries, severe postoperative menopause, the diagnosis of melanoma in her right arm, the diagnosis of throat cancer, the diagnosis of colon cancer, complications of neurosurgery leading to meningitis and finally, just for good measure, a Pontine stroke leading to the loss of function of her dominant arm and leg.

She knew that her recovery would never be complete. She knew that every day would be a struggle to get out of bed, brush her teeth, put on her clothes, go to the bathroom and perform countless activities of daily living that we all take for granted. Despite all of these obstacles, she persevered. She worked diligently at rehabilitation. Each day challenged her resolve to walk a little bit farther; to become a little bit more independent. Progress was agonizingly slow. She then developed life-threatening multi-lobar pneumonia. She was hospitalized for weeks. Her hard won gains had been lost. It was then back to rehabilitation once again to try to regain her lost independence. It was later during her continued recovery at home that she suffered a tragic fall resulting in the fracture of both of her legs and the return once again to rehabilitation.

The term perseverance really does not even begin to describe Regina's journey. She remains warm. She remains hopeful. Her faith in God, her faith in the power of positive energy, her resilience and indeed her remarkable resourcefulness has inspired countless family members, friends, therapists, physicians and many others too countless to name.

In looking back on my journey with Regina and in looking forward to working with her in recovery, I am reminded of the very powerful words spoken by Sam Berns at his Tedx talk several years ago. Sam suffered from a rare genetic disorder called Progeria. His life was tragically cut short as a complication of this rare disease. Nonetheless, he remained remarkably upbeat in his approach to life. Despite multiple physical limitations, he noted that an important part of his philosophy for a happy life was to "be okay with what you ultimately can't do because there is much that you can do."

Regina inspires us through her perseverance and her willingness to share her story. She challenges us not to dwell on what we can't do, but to focus like a laser on those things we can do. If we follow her lead, there is so much that we can accomplish with our lives.

She has inspired me to be a better person and a better physician.

CONTENTS

1

"It is only in our darkest hours that we may discover the true strength of the brilliant light within ourselves that can never, ever, be dimmed."
– Doe Zantamata

Preface

Where Do I Begin?
(Sounds like a good opening line for a hit song, no?)

I must have been one unbelievable batter in a previous life! I say this not to boast of my athletic prowess, but rather to better attempt to convey an image of the significant challenges I have had to face. There have been an incredible variety of health-related pitches thrown at me and not only have I handled them all, but I keep stepping up to the plate. This is not a character element given to me alone. It is inherent within each one of us.

Why me?! *Don't we all ask ourselves that at some point throughout our life's journey?* But if you listen closely, "**Why not me**" has usually been the immediate reply --- at least, it has been for me.

I was born of strong Irish-Portuguese stock, extroverted and fearless, with childhood stories that would make any parent cringe. One day when I was 10, my mother need the rent from the tenants before my father got home but was too afraid to ask for it. So I marched right down the stairs to ask for it myself! When the female tenant tried to close the door in my face, mumbling something about waiting for her husband (it was actually her lover), I stuck my foot in the door and refused to leave until I got it.

I also had no problem getting myself to Mass every Sunday at 5 years of age. Being an early riser, unlike my siblings and parents, I'd put on my Sunday best and off to church I'd go, waiting patiently at the lights to cross Route 16 safely. I'd arrive at least a half an hour early so I could hear the choir, watch the priest set up and have my alone time with God. Little did I comprehend how the wise insight I would receive would build character and help sustain me through all my health challenges some 49 years later.

I want to emphasize that everyone's life experiences and trials are uniquely their own and should be respected as such. This book is not intended to offer definitive answers to everyone's life challenges, only how one simple gal dealt with hers, and how the lessons I have learned may help others. I firmly believe that only with God's help and perseverance have I survived countless health challenges --- among them, four cancers, a brain cyst, a Pontine stroke, and double-pneumonia. Yes, faith is a large component throughout this book. Science, as well, has indeed played a substantial part in my overcoming such adversities. Faith -- in oneself and in an external being (God, Creator, external life force or whatever your definition is) -- rules the day. Within these pages is my quest to find some answers for myself to the questions regarding adversity we all must face in this life. Let the two-finger, right-handed typing begin!

Now, where on earth do I start?

Chapter 1 - Seriously? Seriously!

Bad things do happen; how I respond to them defines my character and the quality of my life. I can choose to sit in perpetual sadness, immobilized by the gravity of my loss, or I can choose to rise from the pain and treasure the most precious gift I have - life itself.
Walter Anderson[2]

Are you kidding me? That was my initial thought as I stumbled, grabbing the pole just outside my apartment bathroom where my dear friend, Hunter, was sitting with his son Nathan, a senior in high school. (They had witnessed death firsthand before with the loss of their wife and mother who was also my dearest friend.) "Not again," I prayed silently, as I stumbled out of the bathroom calling to Hunter. "Help me," I prayed and hoped for as I grasped the pole to avoid landing in a heap on the floor. Little did I know that I was in the beginning stages of a life threatening stroke.

I was living in a bucolic enclave, but you could drive down the hill and you found yourself smack dab in the middle of the hustle and bustle of urban life. This enclave is so set back that finding the 2nd last house on that dead-end street was hindered because even police and rescue didn't know of its existence. My apartment consisted of the lower level of a single family home built on the side of a ledge. This didn't make it any easier for me to drag myself up the narrow flight of stairs to get to ground level where the EMTs could evacuate me to the hospital. Time was of the essence. I've since learned the true significance of **F. A. S. T**. I hope we all learn to think:

> **F**-Facial drooping,
> **A**-Arm Weakness,
> **S**-Speech difficulties;
> **T**-Time.

Never in my wildest dreams had I imagined the need to endure yet another potential life-threatening health situation, yet another challenge I would have to overcome if I wanted to live. What was this all about? What now?!

Let's review for a moment, shall we? Starting in 2001 to present, I have endured the following:

- Breast Cancer-*check*,
- Chronic Cellulitis-*check*,
- Melanoma-*check*,
- Throat Cancer-*check*,
- Back Surgery-*check*,
- Rectal Cancer-*check*,
- Brain Cyst-*check*,
- Stroke-*check*,
- Double Pneumonia, on life support-*check*,
- Two broken legs-*check*.

Not a bucket list I would have made for myself, believe you me, but as my sister rightly put into context, "We all have our own life challenges." And here was another one.

Good Lord, what could be next?

Chapter 2 - Death Of My Twin

Batter Up: 1st Inning

It's 1996 and my life's going great! Thirty-three years old and I'm lovin' God, life, and enjoying school as a "returning student". I'm livin' my dreams --- singing liturgical music with Christopher Walker[3]; serving as his backup cantor at Saint Paul the Apostle Church in Westwood, CA at the 9:30 a.m. Sunday Mass; lending my voice on liturgical music recordings for Walker and the Saint Thomas More Group (various composers from England on Oregon Catholic Press); participating in various diocesan, regional and national events; and cantoring at Good Shepherd Church in Beverly Hills, CA and living on campus at Mount Saint Mary's College in nearby Brentwood, CA.

During my first week as a junior in college, life changed for good. Challenges to my character and faith would be tested time and again.

On a balmy, late summer's evening I collapsed onto the bed in my semi-private dorm room at Mount Saint Mary's College finding it hard to breath The only thing I remember thinking was, *Once I open my eyes, everything will be ok.* Really, I thought nothing of it and went about my studies. Just an odd episode, I thought to myself. Little did I realize that at that very instant my twin brother, Richard, was dying by drowning 3,000 miles away.

Fast forward 34 hours. I took my early morning swim in the Mount's outside pool surrounded by a beautiful backdrop of nature at the top of the Santa Monica Mountains overlooking the Pacific Ocean with deer staring back at me. I finished my morning exercise ritual, showered, readying myself for the joys of what I'd be learning next, and headed to my 6 a.m. job opening the campus gym.

I had been at work no more than 30 minutes when my cell phone rang; Aunt Mary was calling. *That's odd*, I wondered, *how did she get my cell number?* She told me there's a "possible issue" with Richard, and "they're hoping he may be heading my way so be on the lookout for him just in case." Completely confused, I hung up the phone but those words kept haunting me.

About 30 minutes or so later, I called back to try to get some further clarification. Aunt Kathleen answered and tried to say something but she was crying too hard and not making any sense. She handed the phone to Aunt Mary who, while trying to control her voice, finally said those crushing words every family member dreads hearing: **"Richard's gone."**

Now I'm thoroughly confused. *Gone? Gone where?"*

"He's dead!" she replied.

Silence can indeed be deafening.

Even though we were twins, we were the epitome of polar opposites, or so some would think. Richard was the quiet, deep thinker. I was outgoing, spontaneous, and gregarious. He would come up with the ingenious schemes and I would execute them. There were times when it didn't turn out in my favor, yet I trusted him implicitly.

Yes, opposites. But I suggest that polar opposites are complementary in nature. Shadows cannot, after all, exist without light. One element might be stronger at times, as it was with Richard and I. But that only strengthened our bond. Let something or someone just try to come between us, and one would invariably not be happy with the outcome.

And now my brother was gone.

Alone in the gym, overcome by grief, I broke down. Then I hung up the phone, closed the gym and stepped outside. I looked up to the heavens where I was treated to one of the most beautiful sunrises I had ever experienced. As I walked to the chapel, I looked eastward, towards home, and saw a lone bird flying towards the sunrise. *Head home to God, Richard* was all I could think of at that moment.

Searching for a new beginning, Richard had relocated to the West Coast. There we could support each other again in closer proximity. Gone for a short time was our bi-coastal communications. While living in L.A., Richard tried to make his way in the art world. But he didn't like always being mistaken for his idol Jim Morrison. He was often called out for closely resembling him, however. In one instance while he was out to dinner with his friends from the East Coast, a spotlight suddenly appeared on him with the DJ proclaiming, "Jim Morrison is in 'da house!" Being the introvert, Richard was mortified with all the attention drawn to him.

Richard also despised earthquakes. He didn't care much for snow either, but he could tolerate a snow-covered ground more than the unexpected, shaking ground underfoot, so in less than 6 months later after a minor earthquake, Richard took flight back to Boston, MA. I don't remember ever seeing him alive after that.

The Long Journey Home

My emotional journey home began with a red-eye trip from L.A. home to Boston to say goodbye. Only large events remain in my memory after that. The rest is a complete blur. I know that I immediately went into my professional, autopilot mode, trying, sometimes in vain, to control myself in order to get through what awaited:

- Cleaning out his private living space of regular, guy stuff, something parents shouldn't have to wade through. The entire time I was mentally reassuring him, *I've got your back, Bro.*
- Picking up Richard's clothing remains from the funeral home, (his other possessions were never found).
- Helping to organize his funeral mass, which included creating the worship aid and singing (more on that in a moment).
- Because police classified his death as drowning in the river and the cause of death was questioned as a potential murder, we had to meet two times with the police.
- Flying back to L.A.

All of this took place within one week. That was the condition the college placed on me so as to not to completely miss my new semester.

The funeral mass seemed surreal to me. I'd sung at countless weddings and funerals since I was 16, but I had never imagined I would be singing at my own twin brother's funeral at age 33. But being an extroverted, ultra Type A personality allowed me to get through the mass, as did my profound belief in the ultimate resurrection of the human soul. Richard had once told me jokingly that I only really sounded great in church. Now his words only made me more determined to do a good job, allowing my parents, sisters, family and friends to celebrate Richard's life and send him to his heavenly home singing and praising God.

Once back in California, I brought some flowers and dirt I'd taken from Richard's gravesite and drove directly to Venice Beach. I parked just outside the facility Richard had worked at (near the shore's edge), walked towards the water, rolled up my pants, and walked into the Pacific, where I released the flowers and sand. As I walked quietly back to the shore, alone in my thoughts, a woman I'd never seen came over and, without saying a word, hugged me tightly.

Remember Me

We were blessed to receive at least two signs of Richard's salvation. A few months after he died, Richard's best friend, Arthur, called me in California to tell me of his reoccurring dream. In most of his dreams, Richard would not acknowledge Arthur's presence; but in the most recent dream, Richard had turned to face Arthur, who asked Richard directly what had happened.

"I don't know what is happening," Richard replied, "but once I open my eyes, everything will be OK." It was the exact phrase I had heard in my own mind at the exact moment Richard was dying.

Richard, Arthur told me, then smiled. Behind him, stood Jesus with his arm around Richard's shoulder.

The other sign we realized in the process of cleaning out Richard's living space. We discovered three huge pictures of Jesus and Mary he had created, as well as hundreds of poems he'd written throughout his life. The images -- one of them done in charcoal from floor to ceiling -- were in various stages of progress, or perhaps they were completed. We'll never know. I do know, however, that they are truly inspiring images to people who asked for a private viewing in my former single family home. There they viewed them, and sat in quiet reflection. They now reside in a public chapel in Boston where so many more can appreciate his art. I have entitled this work, *For Our Sins.*[4]

You see, God blessed both of us with different artistic talents. Twenty years after Richard returned to his heavenly home, his poetry, art and music continues to touch thousands of people in over 35 countries --- from Namibia to the Netherlands, India to Ireland, Japan to Iran and every state in the U.S. Feel free to visit https://www.facebook.com/PoetsCorner-RichardsOriginals.

"If you are going through hell, keep going."
~ ***Winston Churchill***

Think About It

Have you ever endured a significant loss?
Think about your reaction.
What was your response?
Were you angry at God or did you find solace from Him?
Did you turn the negative into a positive?

Chapter 3 – Breast Cancer

Batter Up: 2nd Inning

After Richard's death, I made a conscious choice to return home to Boston from Los Angeles in 1997 after I had graduated, to help my aging parents. My parents were then in their 50s, which at the time I thought was old (crazy me. I'm of that age right now and I'm not old.) I was single, and both my sisters had families and young children to care for. I thought the best way to give back to my parents, for all that they had sacrificed for my siblings and me during our formative years, was to return home.

I returned to my former place of employment that need support, a job I enjoyed, and I regained health insurance. Since it had been a few years since my last full checkup, I decided to get one. My new PCP recommended a baseline mammogram. *No problem,* I thought; it was a good idea to be proactive.

Layoffs occurred about a year and a half later, so last in, first out. I was again looking for a job while temping when, after several months, much to my surprise, the HR rep called, offering another permanent job administrating the quality department. I love quality work. It was a great fit.

It was now two years since my baseline mammogram and because I once again had insurance, I scheduled another exam which included a mammogram. Little did I envision the medical roller coaster ride ahead of me.

Snap Shot in Time

"Miss Pontes," the technician called out my name for the THIRD time due to questionable mammograms. "Can you come with me? The radiologist needs to speak to you."

I followed her into in a small, darkened room sitting with only the doctor and negative images of my breasts staring back at me. The doctor informed me there was a questionable area in my right breast and that I need to go directly to the Burlington location of Lahey Clinic[5] for a more thorough examination and testing. I vividly remember being annoyed and thinking, *I'm too busy at work to have to do this right now.*

But I knew something was up even as I gathered my belongings for the trip to Burlington. An older lady in the waiting room stared at me, crying. Trying to ease her pain, I said, "Now I know just how Cindy Crawford[6] feels." I gave her a hug and proceed to Burlington.

Once at the main hospital, I was led through the hallway with still pictures staring back at me. When will this end? I wondered in an annoyed manner. *I've got to return to work.* That thought was abruptly cut short when the oncologist called me in and confirmed, in a matter-of-fact way, "We think you have cancer. We need to perform a biopsy to truly get the answer, though." Her tone was caring, but her words were very direct.

I looked at her, both bewildered and annoyed, because I had not yet accrued any vacation time. *Great*, I lamented, *another day down the toilet.*

The biopsy confirmed the diagnosis. It was 9 p.m., Holy Thursday when the doctor called with the news. My biopsy results were in and I had breast cancer.

Who's Got Time For This?!

My initial internal reaction upon hearing the news was defiance. *I don't have time to deal with this right now.* But I was in shock, too. My family took it harder than I since I was only the second family member at that time having to deal with this diagnosis, one of my mother's sisters being the first years earlier. My sister even came straight over to me that night, not wanting to leave my side. At 11.30 p.m. that night, I finally had to kick her out so we could both get some much need sleep.

As a control freak, Type A personality, this was unfamiliar territory to me, both my illness and my lack of control over the impending situation. Good Friday services struck me deeply the next day. Would this be my sacrifice? Would I be with Jesus and Richard this time next Good Friday? That Easter Sunday, I planted perennial flowers, thinking that if I wasn't here next year, something would still blossom and grow in my place.

At the following Monday consultation at the breast cancer clinic, the oncologist told me in a direct, monotone voice that I had a 1-centimeter tumor -- right on the cusp of needing all three modalities of treatment. Had it been 1.01

or more in diameter, gone would have been my ability to choose one of the three modalities I was given:

1. Lumpectomy alone = 90% survival rate.
2. Lumpectomy with radiation. = 94% survival rate
3. Lumpectomy, radiation and chemotherapy = 94.5% survival rate.

For a second, I thought I was ordering a pizza with toppings or playing *Let's Make A Deal,* as in, *I'll take what's behind door number 2, Doctor. I'll die 6 months earlier.*

One lumpectomy and two margin excisions later, the doctor was still trying to get clean margins but the situation appeared bleak. Finally, I told the doctor, "Look, I'm not using this breast so if you end up not getting clean margins this time, remove the breast."

On the day of the surgery, I surprised the doctor by drawing a smiley face on it just to make sure if he need to remove the breast, he'd remove the correct one. The third time was indeed a charm since he didn't need to completely remove it. Radiation was another matter.

Unfortunately my mother's Irish, fair-skinned genes won out over my father's Portuguese makeup. What should have taken a month or so of radiation in between work turned into six months at home, all the while trying to deal with the radiation and skin constantly burning off. Thank God my employer and co-workers were so patient with my situation.

If I wasn't going for radiation treatment, I was lying down while holding my big breast up in the air. My entrepreneurial spirit kicked in as I created for myself what

I affectionately called the "boob sling", allowing air to get at burnt skin to heal it while giving my arm a badly need rest.

Yes, humor plays an integral part in one's ability to deal with a difficult situation. Throughout her best-seller, *"Don't Leave Me This Way: Or When I Get Back on My Feet You'll Be Sorry!"* Julia Fox Garrison coined the phrase, "Humor Ultimately Gives Strength!" Amen to that, I say daily!

Because my cancer was estrogen receptive, doctors strongly recommended an Oophorectomy (oh-of-uh-REK-tuh-me), the removal of both ovaries and uterus. This procedure was done prophylacticly to avoid ovarian or uterine cancer. Little did I comprehend the off-the-cuff remark, "You'll experience menopausal symptoms after that" -- an understatement for sure, and quite a life changing event at 38 years of age. Although I was still relatively young enough to have children by natural means, that option was now completely off the table. Even though I never had imagined myself as a mother (just "the cool aunt"), it was like having the door slammed in my face. After the surgery, the doctor reminded me that women my age undergoing a hysterectomy and Oophorectomy experience hot flashes 10 times the normal rate that naturally occur. I stand now in solidarity with my northeast menopausal sisters when I say the colder it gets outside, the more comfortable I feel with these hot flashes. I will never forget returning to work six months later, on a bitterly cold, January 2014 morning. I loved being back at work but those damn hot flashes were killing me. Imagine -- right in the middle of an important meeting in the dead of winter and I'm sweating profusely. A VP eyeing my anguish jumped up and proceed to open a window in the conference room proclaiming he was hot.

Thank God I thought to myself while all the other men put on their coat jackets. Needless to say, the meeting was one of the fastest in Arthur D. Little, Incorporated's 130-year company history.

On a more serious note, I would add this: because I have a family history of breast and colon cancer like my sisters and mother along with her siblings, I have become extremely vigilant about my health.

Think About It

Has there ever been a time when you were uncertain of your future?
What steps did you intentionally take to attempt to control and change the course of the direction before you?

Chapter 4 - Death of My BFF

Batter Up: 3rd Inning

Being a trained fashion designer, Nancy was extremely curious to meet the crazy-looking lady who had started her first day on the job wearing a gray-striped business suit and carrying a huge, faux leather, cheap red bag. I was thinking I looked ever-so-fashionable and chic -- *the bomb,* even. In reality I must have looked like a hot mess. No matter; Nancy and I became BFFs to the max.

Even when I moved to L.A. we talked daily, even several times a day, on the phone. She was the first person I called when my brother died and we prayed together. We enjoyed tons of fun and laughs together whenever we could -- celebrations, church functions, social events, family get-togethers. We both tried in vain to learn to ski (big failure, but tons of fun), we double-dated, we shopped. Her back door and pantry window faced my front door, and many a morning she'd signal to me by raising her pantry blind so that we could go walking at 5:30 a.m. The 3,000 miles in between us could not break our bond. So it was unbelievable to me when her brother Mark told me that she died during the night from ovarian cancer.

I had seen her just three days prior when we planned a trip to Lourdes, France. I knew she wasn't feeling well because her husband Hunter said she was sick and couldn't come to the phone, but I never imagined this. We had attended a Divine Mercy event just a week earlier. Now Nancy, one of my few rocks, was gone! Nancy really thought she had a handle on this wretched disease. She even thought she might have become pregnant and was delighted, until the doctor told her that she had ovarian cancer.

Hunter and Danny were two of the best men a woman could know. Ever the organic-centered family, they tried anything and everything to help her. They sought out Eastern and Western medicines to keep her alive, especially for the sake of her beloved children Pauline (12), Anna (10) and Nathan (just shy of 8). Nathan made his first communion only a month before his eighth birthday, but what should have been a time of celebration turned instead into a mass honoring all of Nancy's contributions to the church, with many craftworks she'd made with her loving hands adorning the altar.

Unbroken Bonds

Now two of the most important people in my life had been ripped out from under me --- my brother at 33 and my best friend at 42. Initially I was so very angry at God for allowing this. I was in a lot of emotional pain. My soul mates were both ripped away from me in such an abrupt manner that I could only ultimately rely on God. Once again I relied on that inner voice that intuitively reaffirmed for me that God would never leave my side. It was then that I declared my commitment to follow God no matter what challenges I would endure. I would rely on no other but Him.

Both Richard and Nancy were indeed what Kristin Chenoweth sings about in "Borrowed Angel"[7], which perfectly fits these two loving souls called home. Keep in mind, however, that there really are no coincidences in this life!

Borrowed Angels

Refrain

There must be Borrowed Angels, here in this life
They come along, into this world
and make this world bright
But they can't stay forever
Cause they're heaven sent
And sometimes, heaven needs them back again

Think About It

Has there ever been a soul-mate in your life?
How did you keep the relationship going even after their departure from your life?

Chapter 5 – Chronic Cellulitis

Batter Up: 4th Inning

Over the next several years after the breast cancer surgery, I was affected countless times with varying degrees of cellulitis, which can occur when the lymphatic system is compromised. If immediate medical response is not sought, this disease can kill a person.

My first bout with cellulitis happened in the middle of the night. I awoke suddenly to an agonizing, burning pain in my right arm. This, I believe, was the result of having to endure an axillary node biopsy under my arm where they removed 13 lymph nodes from under my armpit. It is important to note here that while the new normal practice is to do a sentinel node biopsy (where they only remove the three closest nodes that pick up the dye they inject into you), the previous practice was the auxillary procedure. I remember vehemently arguing with the surgeon about how many lymph nodes to remove as I was wheeled into the operating room for the removal of the 13 -- but alas, I lost that battle. He did an axillary node biopsy, removing 16 lymph nodes instead of the 3 sentinel node biopsy option. Thank God this doctor stopped focusing on breast cancer and moved into another specialty that I can only hope suits him better. I hope he learned something from that whole unfortunate experience.

Sadly, cellulitis reoccurred many times in the following years. I became so used to what they would do that I even began drawing with a marker around the area so I could show them just how fast it had grown from the first time I experienced it till the time they finally saw me. Sad, really. In one instance, a myriad of specialists considered the possibility of amputating my right arm to stop the disease from becoming septic which could have killed me.

I was blissfully unaware that I had to turn a proverbial corner in 8 hours or they would perform the amputation! My lymphedema specialist even came over to try to perform some lymph-draining message therapy. Later on she told me she had never really seen my arm, so big that it resembled the size of my thigh. One thing I will never forget is when my PCP informed me that this was very close to experiencing a flesh-eating bacteria. As a result of these experiences, I now have to take a prophylactic antibiotic daily to avoid this disease from reoccurring.

Lesson Learned:
Always communicate your wishes beforehand if you have an opinion! Never feel intimidated by a doctor. Ultimately it is your decision alone. It is your body which has to deal with any negative ramifications, even if there was no intent to harm you. You need to be your own vocal advocate. If you can't for some reason, find a family member or close friend to advocate on your behalf.

Chapter 6 - Melanoma

Batter Up: 5th Inning

What is that raised red spot on my right arm? I wondered. During my exam, I brought it to the doctor's attention.

"I don't think it's a problem," she stated, "but let me take a little sample and have it tested."

I was not worried because it looked like an eraser that you see at the top of a pencil. My only concern was that it was on my right arm where cellulitis kept reoccurring and I was always told emphatically not to allow any blood pressure tests, blood draws, puncture wounds or cuts to the affected arm. In other words, baby it!

The no-nonsense doctor had already spoken to me about watching out for moles that change color. When I dutifully called back later for the findings of the biopsy, she informed me, "It's in the early stage of cancer, a form of melanoma". The dermatologist made an appointment for me to see a surgeon. I ended up undergoing two surgeries to remove the mass and get clean margins yet again.

I was beginning to see a pattern here. Other than the scars that remain, I was told to watch my arm for cellulitis because of the repeated cutting to my arm. I returned back to work. Six months later, so too did the melanoma.

Another go-round with this, and I was thankfully done. As I was leaving, I was told to vigilantly watch it and stay out of the sun. Again, it seems I had inherited my mother's Irish complexion, not my dad's Portuguese genes.

"Perseverance is a positive, active characteristic. It is not idly, passively waiting and hoping for some good thing to happen. It gives us hope by helping us realize that the righteous suffer no failure except in giving up and no longer trying. We must never give up, regardless of temptations, frustrations, disappointments, or discouragements."
~ Joseph P. Wirthlin

Chapter 7 - Throat Cancer

Batter Up: 6th Inning

Because singing had been such an integral part of my life, I have always been extremely aware of my voice and anything else related to my body. I had been singing professionally since the age of 16. Now, at the age 45, I found myself in the waiting room of an otolaryngologist filling out a huge questionnaire.

Are you this or that? Have you done thus and such? Taken who knows what, etc.? I thought, *(Hey, Doc, FYI, this is getting extremely personal!)* I began to wonder about the validity of what seemed like some very invasive questions when I remembered, Note to self, *you came here of your own volition seeking answers to your on-and-off hoarseness and raspiness in your voice. Bare with it.*

A camera tube was placed up my nose and down my throat (not pleasant). Holding on to my friend's hand, the doctor was not happy when my friend looked behind me at the monitor and blurted out, "Yuck, is that mono?" (Boy if looks could kill, I thought my friend Patti would have been dead before she hit the floor.)

The doctor removed the camera and, looking directly at me, asked what brought me here. I told him. He paused, then proceed to tell me just how lucky I was being so attuned to my body. He told me I had throat cancer which is normally not found until it's in a much more advanced and deadly stage. The good thing, he added, is that "you will probably only lose your singing ability."

Good thing? Is he kidding? Seriously?

He was right. The day of the surgery arrived and as I walked into Lahey Clinic, I asked my friend Patti to take me to their chapel. Alone with my thoughts while listening to the instrumental version of David Haas' "You Are Mine[8]," I thanked God for the gift I was given and hoped I had done exactly what the Creator had desired. I came out of surgery with my right vocal cord paralyzed in the open position. Again it reaffirmed for me just who was in charge, teaching me to let go of my uber Type A lifestyle and focus on Him alone, which was hard, to be honest.

I always thought of myself as humble, but this catapulted me into a whole new realm. Having been able to sing even before I could speak made this permanent change in my life completely earth-shattering. Think for a moment of the one thing that had brought you the most comfort, the most "self identifying" thing about you, a true piece of your soul --- and then rip it out in one instant. My identity was gone! Only questions remained, and may very well remain until my last breath.

You Are Mine

I will come to you in the silence
I will lift you from all your fear
You will hear My voice
I claim you as My choice
Be still, and know I am near

I am hope for all who are hopeless
I am eyes for all who long to see
In the shadows of the night,
I will be your light
Come and rest in Me

Refrain

Do not be afraid I am with you
I have called you each by name
Come and follow Me
I will bring you home
I love you and you are mine

I am strength for all the despairing
Healing for the ones who dwell in shame
All the blind will see, the lame will all run free
And all will know My name *to refrain*

I am the Word that leads all to freedom
I am the peace the world cannot give
I will call your name, embracing all your pain
Stand up now, walk, and live *to refrain*

25

For my rendition of this song and other liturgical songs and secular music, feel free to visit www.soundcloud.com/rmmp62

"A difficult time can be more readily endured if we retain the conviction that our existence holds a purpose — a cause to pursue, a person to love, a goal to achieve."
~ John Maxwell

Think about It

Have you ever felt so strongly about something you identified with that you felt lost without it? Were you able to begin to focus yourself on another God-given skill that you possess?

Chapter 8 - Hemilaminectomy, Adenoidectomy and Rectal Cancer

Batter Up: 7th Inning Stretch

Having a family history of breast and colon cancer via my sisters, I became extremely vigilant about my health and I try to incorporate my experiences to good use addressing my needs.

In the summer of 2008, I was minding my own business just washing the cars on a beautiful Sunday morning in New England. Unfortunately, the next morning, I awoke with the worst pain I have ever experienced. I normally have a high tolerance for pain, but this was excruciating! The pain ran from my lower back all the way down to my kneecap. I swear, I was going to rip my kneecap off at any minute.

Unfortunately my PCP's schedule was completely booked, but the pain was so severe I couldn't wait, so I saw his P.A. Thank God. did because I had two badly ruptured disks, requiring immediate back surgery.

After the surgery, I awoke in the recovery room. My agonizing pain was now replaced by simple surgical recovery pain. *I can deal with this,* I thought. Since there were no rooms available in the hospital, I stayed the night in a dimly lit space in the corner of the recovery unit. There, I was attended to by Maria, one of two nurses to care for the four patients that remained. I quietly praised and thanked God for gifting my doctors and nurses thus allowing for a successful surgical outcome.

I spontaneously began softly singing "Amazing Grace." The nurse, Maria, heard me. She quietly approached and began harmonizing with me to the song. The janitor overheard us while mopping the floor and also harmonized in Haitian. Finally, we finished the song in perfect harmony, and all was quiet. We stared smiling back at each other silently acknowledging this "God Moment."

Later that year, during a regularly scheduled colonoscopy due to a family history of colon cancer, doctors found a small, questionable mass within my rectal cavity. They tried twice to properly remove it, but tissue is limited in that area. Off I went to a rectal surgeon.

The specialist informed me that he was going to have to do surgery. Worst case scenario, I would wake up with a colostomy bag since a good amount of tissue had already been removed in the last two attempts. Needless to say, undergoing these prep tests meant that all semblance of modesty flew out the window!

I was sick and tired of cancer! "Listen doctor," I said. "Before you do this procedure, I want a PET scan. **IF ANYTHING LIGHTS UP LIKE A CHRISTMAS TREE, TAKE IT OUT!**" He readily agreed, knowing my history. What a doll!

The results told me that not only did the questionable area light up but there were also questionable areas near my tonsils and adenoids. "Then I want a two-fer," I said. The doctor looked at me quizzically but agreed to a tag-team operation with the doctor who had previously performed the throat cancer. (On surgery day, I chuckled at the prep nurse's confusion when she saw that I was in for a colorectal/tonsil/adenoidectomy.)

Know what the worst part of this recovery was? I'll give you two tries and the first one doesn't count. My throat was killing me. I was in so much pain, I gladly took Roxicet. I even wrote an "Ode to Roxicet," sung to the tune of "We Love You Conrad" from Bye Bye Birdie.[9]

I love you Roxicet,
Oh yes I do
You take my pain away
and make me loopy too
When you're not with me, I'm blue
Oh Roxicet I love you!
(I guess I could have been classified as medically
stoned while wring these lyrics.)

Needless to say, my boss wasn't laughing when he tried to conduct an audit with me over the phone. Poor Art! That audit didn't last long or go well at all.

Chapter 9 - Rathkye Brain Cyst and Meningitis

Batter Up: 8th Inning

What's up with my eyes? I thought while trying to work on my resume, updating my LinkedIn profile and checking my emails after just being laid off. *This blurriness is odd*, so I found myself schlepping off yet again to Lahey. This was starting to feel like my second home, though I would rather have a beach front home in Maine.

By now, I had amassed an excellent medical team. After reviewing the MRI they requested, the chairman of Neurosurgery department discovered what he thought was a tumor pressing on my optic nerve. He told me that with my history he need to consult with the chairman of the Ear, Nose and Throat (ENT) department. Result: I would require surgery with the chairmen of both the Neurological and ENT departments participating. They need to extract the tumor by going up through my nose to reach the correct location. At least, the scar would be hidden (unlike all the others). Because this happened right after my layoff, I was still under insurance, thank God. I kept thinking, *Thank you Keenan[10]*.

All was going well in surgery until the robotic machine the doctors were using grabbed the tumor. To their surprise, the tumor exploded with fluid the consistency of motor oil. They told me it was good news that it wasn't actually a tumor, but rather they reclassified it as a cyst. They advised me to watch out for a spinal leak, which would be serious, and sent me on my merry way. I was told to go home to heal. During the weekly post operative recovery, I continually had an innate sense that something was amiss. I felt an overwhelming sense that this struggle wasn't going to be that easily resolved. Again, I dutifully abided by my post operative instruction and sent home, yet still felt an inner uneasiness. My instinct proved itself correct a few days later.

I kept trying to convince myself that the doctors packed that area well. Unfortunately within the week I was again rushed back into the emergency room with a splitting headache and I had become completely photophobic (any light was unbearable). As an added "bonus," there were so many patients in the waiting room and ER that they stuck me on a gurney in the hallway next to the bathroom. All I asked for was something to cover my head to keep out the light!

Unbeknownst to me, my sister and mother had arrived and began searching for me in the ER. My sister was floored when she heard where I was and demanded to have me seen in minutes (God bless her!). Patty may not raise her voice but she gets her point across and people listen.

They ended up admitting me yet again and I was there for a week because they realized I had a really bad case of meningitis! Even with the battery of doctors I saw during that week, consisting of 3 teams of 7 doctors, they all missed one critical point until the day before they were to send me home.

Being a quality control person by profession, I'm cognizant of the protocols of performing a root-cause analysis. So I asked a simple question: "Why has no one bothered to look up at the surgical area?" There were 21 doctors, residents and trainees and all of them stared at me in bewilderment -- and, I would think, embarrassment. "I don't know", was the only reply one resident finally muttered. "Seriously?" I replied **SERIOUSLY?!?!**

In the afternoon the day before they planned to release me they sent me down to the ENT department. It didn't take very long for the resident to unpack the surgical area before they realized I did, in fact, have a spinal fluid leak and Meningitis was present. Let's just say I was overcome by this entire event.

So the next day, instead of going home, the doctors prepared me for yet another surgery -- this time to repair the hole they all had previously missed! Once that procedure was over, I stayed for another few days just to be certain all was clear. Right before I left the ENT doctor, he said "You're one lucky lady. If you hadn't spoken up we wouldn't have searched that area and you would have been one sick lady for a long time"!

Yeah, right, I thought. I firmly believe that I was led to the right answer by the one, true, real physician and healer of all humanity, Jesus Christ.

Now back to the job at hand: finding a new job

Chapter 10 - Pontine Stroke

OK, no disrespect here to Job of the Scriptures, but I'm beginning to feel a real kinship with this guy right about now!

Batter Up: 9th Inning

Hurricane Irene was slated to hit land on Sunday, August 12, 2011 in the Boston area. The day before, not wishing to have my lawn furniture used as mini-missiles rocketing onto my neighbors' property, my friend Hunter and his son Nathan came over to help me move the outdoor furniture inside and watch a movie. With such dear friends, all I can say is that I'm one of the luckiest girls on earth!

The previous Monday I had almost taken a dive, or "took a Dixie," as we say on the East Coast. I never really fell down during my accident, I just caught myself against the bureau and wall; my head moving as if I was getting whiplash in a car accident. But other than a badly-bruised ego, that was it as far as being injured. I brushed myself off and went to work. I honestly thought nothing of it after that.

That Friday I put down a $1,000 deposit to purchase an upscale Camp Ellis beach house only three houses from the ocean in Saco, Maine. Life was taking a positive turn, I thought. Fun times lay ahead on this balmy, late Saturday summer's evening. Let's watch a movie!

OK, so I did have a broken toe and a constant low-grade headache after my "near-Dixie", yet I truly thought nothing of it. My mother, however, convinced me to have both issues looked at, so off I went to the doctor's office. I was unfortunately unable to see my PCP that Friday (August 10), so I made an appointment with an associate of his.

We talked about the fall and the resulting two issues. He then sent me down to x-ray to have my foot examined and stay down there when I was done so he could address the second issue. After the x-ray, he informed me that he thought my headache resulted from a low-grade sinus infection and prescribed the necessary nasal spray. Off I went to work.

On Saturday, August 11, Hunter, Nathan and I enjoyed movie and pizza after they helped me prepare my house for impending Hurricane Irene the next day. While watching the movie, my eyes began to burn and become blurry. Now I've got more than a broken toe and a headache to deal with. I told the guys I would lie down in bed for a few minutes. Hunter said he'd check in on me every 20 minutes. I got up several times to use the bathroom. The third time coming out of the bathroom, I collapsed against the supporting beam in the hall. "I can't walk", was all I could say.

Hunter leapt up, grabbed me and tried to help me up the stairs. All I could think of was, *What's happening? Get me to the hospital!* We made it up the majority of stairs only two stairs from the top when I couldn't take it anymore. I simply collapsed on the stair, resting my head on his chest. I yelled for my father to use his lifeline to call an ambulance.

Hunter rode with me in the ambulance to the ER. What happened after is a blur. I remember being wheeled around for a CAT scan and holding on to Hunter's hand as the doctor administered the TPA shot to combat what the doctor believed was an active stroke. I remember the doctor asking me to squeeze Hunter's hand as hard as I could. It felt like a lifetime squeezing his hand, then I simply let go.

That's all I remember. Unbeknownst to me, discussions of a stroke and life and death scenarios were swirling around me. My sister arrived in the ER thinking I was just under the weather. She never envisioned having to make a life or death decision! Upon her arrival, she immediately understood the severity of the situation. The head doctor attempted to care for me while also getting vital information to deal with the situation. Time was of the essence as stroke patients have only a 3 hour window of time to act. The radiologist reading my charts was floored when he relayed his findings. He thought I was either comatose or unfortunately had already succumbed to my stroke. Pontine, or brain stem strokes, debilitate the Pons area of the brain that controls motor skills such as breathing! Of all types of strokes the smallest percentage is Pontine strokes, and only 10% of these stroke victims normally survive.

When it was determined that it was indeed a stroke, the doctor and attending resident ran to my sister telling her that she had literally a minute to determine if I was to receive the TIA shot or just see what would happen. The major consequence was that the shot could also kill me! The resident started to cry softly as my sister pondered her decision and the potential consequences. When my sister asked her why she was so upset, the resident replied that she herself had had to make that same call regarding her own sister which I believe it didn't end favorably.

My sister decided to have the doctor give me the shot and she felt a sense of peace no matter the outcome. The doctor herself ran up to the hospital pharmacy to get the TIA shot. I still had a bit of mobility as I was consciously squeezing Hunter's hand as the doctor inserted the needle. I went unconscious. The situation was touch and go for the following 36 hours. I didn't know the hurricane had skirted our location with only heavy rains to contend with. Hunter still made the cumbersome bus ride to the hospital to make sure I came through. He had gone home to check on his son who was left at home. Once he was assured Nathan was ok, Hunter returned to the hospital. My memory returned a day and a half later. I awoke in the step-down ICU, being attended by two loving nurses. I felt blessed to be in their care.

My discomfort lay in the fact I couldn't move my left side at all, annoying indeed since I was left-handed! Also, one never really thinks about having to rearrange a person's body to take pressure off that area until you can't do it and rearrange that person's position again to prevent otherwise preventable pressure sores. I had to get help for the littlest of things.

God is good though. I was alive. I started to really comprehend just how my life had changed. I knew I wasn't alone. Don't get me wrong. I was upset and I still am when I think of how my life was changed by this freak tripping accident. Ultimately I knew, really KNEW that I was not alone.

I remembered a conversation I had with one of my former professors, Father Jan Michael Joncas[11]. Years earlier he relayed to me his own very personal, life-altering health crisis. The moment was profound. He was stricken with a severe case of Guillian-Barre syndrome. Gone for a time was this vibrant and active priest, professor and liturgical composer ("On Eagles' Wings"), replaced by a physically broken and hemi-paralyzed human being.

Instead of being the one who ministered to the sick and suffering, he found himself on the receiving end of those prayers. What he told me had a deep, philosophical impact on my recovery then and does to this day. Temporarily paralyzed, all he could really do in the hospital was pray for himself. He soon expanded that to include the individuals to his immediate left and right; then expanded even further to include every person on that floor. Ultimately, he found himself praying for those suffering throughout the entire hospital and beyond.

I immediately began to do likewise. Like the good Father Joncas, to this day I ponder, pray for and minister to the sick and suffering through a new lens. It has become a new and fulfilling aspect of my life ministering in my own way through social media. Father Joncas is right too, when he says to this day God continues to remind him, and us all, of the One who's really in charge here.

Baby Steps

During my recovery, I have utilized various in-facility and at-home occupational and physical therapy services including physiatrists (stroke doctors). On the day before leaving one rehab facility, the in-house psychiatrist, who came in to visit me daily at 6:30 a.m., wished me luck. Then, looking at me very seriously, he asked me a question: "How can I bottle up your spirit?"

"I don't know," I replied, smiling.

Then, turning serious, I continued. "All I can say with certainty is that every day, like clockwork, I wake up at 5:30 a.m. and the first thing I think of is to thank God for this day. I then make a conscious choice whether to be happy or sad, mean or jovial for the day. It's much easier to choose to be happy. I could slam my head against a wall but the only outcome would be a splitting headache. Ultimately, it's only through my walk that I have been blessed in this suffering with God."

He wished me God's blessings, smiled, turned and silently left.

There have been struggles for sure, like learning how to write all over again with my NOW dominant right hand. You can imagine how frustrating it has been for a left-handed person to be unable to use a lifeless left hand. Years earlier several of my teachers attempted in vain to convert me to a right-handed person. At nearly 50 years old, I spent countless hours practicing my penmanship like I did when I was 5! My mind kept repeating, like a mantra, "Stay in between the lines."

Yes, there have been many trials and heartaches throughout the following months. The biggest aid in my recovery was the love and support I received from family and friends, augmented by many episodes of laughter (I'll address those later). Gone, or at least minimized, has been my uber-Type-A personality, replaced by a person who tries daily to experience the love of God on a whole new level, one filled with praise for the simple beauty of God's creation all around me. I work out daily, to get out of this wheelchair and eventually use just a walker or a cane! Alas, for now, the electric wheelchair appears to be my current mode of transportation. Along with the new car and lift, I'm learning a new way of becoming more mobile and independent. I recently read a statement that said, rather than think "permanently disabled," think, "I am mobility impaired." My cognitive abilities are as sharp as ever.

Remember, Nathan was not quite 8 years old when his mother Nancy died. Now 22, he is currently my PCA and is going to college, studying to go into the medical profession. Coincidence? You decide. I continue to work and pray every day for myself and others struggling through their illnesses.

> *"The man who removes a mountain begins by carrying away small stones."*
> ~ **Chinese Proverb**

Think About It
What have been the starting over or baby steps in your own life?

Chapter 11 - Double Pneumonia/Life Support

Batter Up: Overtime!

December 5, 2012 was my 50th birthday. *I made it!* I thought, with a smile and a prayer of thanksgiving. *Several more weeks and I can start 2013 off with a bang.*

I had just gone out in public with Hunter for the first time since the stroke to my 30th reunion. We topped it off that Thanksgiving weekend with a non-surprise 50th birthday party. Life was going good! But wait, here we go again.

Dutifully I had the local pharmacist stop by the day before my birthday to give me my yearly flu shot. Less than 12 hours later: birthday bummer! I became extremely ill.

For the next two days, both my mother and sister tried in vain to nurse me back to health. Even calling the doctor and administering Tamaflu™ was useless. Off I went again, barely conscious, to the ER at Lahey Clinic. I was having a hard time trying to even breathe.

By Saturday morning, the doctor informed me that he need to intubate me (inserting breathing and feeding tubes down my throat). Not waiting for my mother and sister to arrive, I gave the doctor and nurse a list of people to contact, jokingly telling them to tell my sister Valerie in Maryland to find me a Vera Wang backless johnnie because it was "all about me" (thank God she got the joke and did find a knockoff). Off I went on another medical odyssey.

Have you ever heard of what the saints refer to as "The Dark Night Of The Soul"? This has indeed been mine, to date anyway! Let me briefly try to explain this concept as described on a site called Catholic Dialogue[12]:

"Christianity is based on relationship – with God and with others. Like all relationships, disillusionment will challenge even the strongest of souls. St. John of the Cross coined the phrase the dark night of the soul to describe the struggle and despair when faith is dry, prayer brings no consolation, and even the existence of God is questioned. The great spiritual writers describe the dark night of the soul as a time of purification, though this brings little comfort to someone who is spiritually depressed. Many of our greatest saints have experienced this darkest of nights. including Mother Teresa of Calcutta and St. Thérèse of Lisieux.

As with a love relationship, we cannot expect to remain in a honeymoon stage of faith. After a deeply spiritual time of retreat, we have to return to the messiness of everyday life. After an intense time of formation, we go forth to live our faith in action only to find our early ideals quickly shattered. Or maybe lethargy and boredom slowly creeps into our body and soul and drains us of all passion, drive and energy.

As with a love relationship, we need to pray for patience and perseverance during the dry times. We need to remind ourselves of why we fell in love (believed) in the first place. We have to work hard at nurturing our faith relationship when the warm fuzzies and emotional highs are gone. We have to keep the lines of communication (prayer) open – especially when we don't feel like talking anymore. And, we should seek help from trained spiritual guides and counselors.

These words ring of platitudes, and I apologize. A few words cannot do justice to the complexity of this topic, and words seldom bring comfort to the soul that is suffering through the dark night. Sometimes all we can do is wait and hope for the light of day to come soon. And, with it, the true joy of a stronger and more mature faith."

I was given Propofol which induces a semi-comatose state. In addition to the breathing and feeding tubes, my sister had also approved of my hands being tethered to the bed rails so I wouldn't inadvertently attempt to remove the breathing tubes with my good hand. I guess that can happen from time to time. So there I was, tied down unable to even perform the simplest act of scratch my nose if need! They woke me up briefly each morning while they determined whether today would be the day the tubes would be removed. If not, then back I went into the induced sleep.

Whenever I was awake, I struggled to breathe. And I prayed, incessantly. Restrained, I could only point to a letter on a clipboard the doctor or nurse held. I remember one occasion where I was ready to give up and told the doctor to just take out the tubes. The resident had entered the room and I motioned to her with my finger relaying that I was both emotionally and physically spent. 'You can let me go' I typed, I was at peace with my decision. She wasn't, however. She kept telling me to hold on just one more day but I had already heard that 6 previous days. I firmly believed that was going to be my final day. She told a little white lie as I still had 3 more days to endure that situation.

The only visitor I allowed was my sister, since my mother already was stressed trying to take care of my ailing father who was suffering from, and ultimately succumbed to Alzheimer's. There was also one visit (God bless them) when my mother, aunt and cousin came to visit me in the ICU. They were chatting and laughing, while I lay there trying just to breathe and stay alive. Trying hard not to laugh, I caught the nurse's attention and motioned to her to kindly kick them out. Yes, I did have them kicked out! I was too busy trying to stay alive, rather than entertaining visitors.

We laugh about it now, but I stayed in that condition for 10 days! At one point I remember begging God to have the doctors remove the tubes and let me go home (and I mean truly home!). I told the resident that we had given it the good old college try, but it wasn't working and I just wanted to go home to God. She didn't listen to me, thank God.

Lying in bed that long not moving a muscle, unfortunately, causes muscles to atrophy. I lost much of the strength and mobility I previously worked so hard to gain back directly after the stroke, which meant I was back at square one. This has been the most frustrating aspect of this struggle so far, trying to relearn yet again to use those muscles. My left hand remains much harder to use now; at times, it's basically like a claw. The tone in both my hand and foot are worse. My foot refuses to this day to lay flat on the floor, still turning in the brace causing constant though mostly tolerable pain with every step I take.

With the therapists and PCA, I continue to work out daily to try to regain my mobility. Remember, I said to myself, *You're Regina, a creation of God and with God's help, you're the little engine that can and will persevere!*

"Never, never, never, never give up."
~ ***Winston Churchill***

Think About It

Have you experienced a Dark Night of the Soul moment? If so, what was your Dark Night of the Soul moment? How did you rebuild your relationship with God?

Chapter 12 - S^!t Happens
(both literally and figuratively)

"Events may be horrible or inescapable.
Men have always a choice -
if not whether,
then how, they may endure."[13]
—*Lois McMaster Bujold*

Batter Up: Post Game Wrap Up

Life exists. So does adversity. The challenge is to face it head-on. That's how we develop our strength and character; that's how we grow as human beings; that's how we can unlock the power within each of us.

It is certainly true that when one's life is on the line, as I have learned only too well, change is inevitable. Some changes are minimal, while others can be daunting, life-altering challenges. Which brings me to some of my challenges that are not, shall we say, a topic of most cocktail party conversations.

I'm talking about bodily functions, and the loss thereof.

My loss of bodily functions, which happens from time to time, can be attributed to my stroke. And while there are several medical alternatives to address this, there is still the psychological matter of coming to terms with this life-altering issue, which by the way, will likely affect most of us, stroke or not, at some point as we get older. (So pay attention!)

Food intake for bodily nutrition needs to be evacuated, right? Well, little did I realize its significance until I was hospitalized and immobile. Gone were worries about singing performances or qualitative analytical, systemic business issues. Now my life revolved around inquisitive nurses and assistants concerned with my regular nutritional input, and output of bodily waste, its density, consistency and quantity.

I was initially mortified, finding this an unnecessary intrusion into a very personal matter (maybe the most personal matter of all), until I realized these actions, once taken for granted, indeed served quite a prominent function. A new mindset was in order.

For starters, it meant modesty flew out the window, especially when I realized that

(a) people just want to help, and

(b) half the population has what I have, body-part speaking, or has seen it. Besides, the medical professionals who deal with this, something which might make the rest of us pass out, picked that field of study, so they know what they're doing, and they are trying to help. So I shouldn't sweat it (and neither should you, should the time ever come.)

Let's be honest here, it wasn't easy to get used to this. There was a time when I had to have a catheter (I affectionately named it "Cathy") removed. What I thought would be a personal matter turned instead into an impromptu party when, after the removal, I need to urinate. Seven people in the room cheered me on, in part because I could do it properly while others couldn't.

When was the last time you celebrated a trip to the bathroom? I truly believe it is important to celebrate even the smallest achievements because others may not have that luxury. Again it comes down to how we deal with the situation at hand. We can struggle and persevere until we break through the proverbial wall (inspired by "Break on Through", by the Doors), or we can engulf ourselves in fear and pity and never get anywhere.

Yes, I still have my fears, but I choose to fight daily to overcome them. I'd rather be known as that wobbly punching bag who never really falls down but bounces right back up, ready for the next challenge, instead of a rock that quietly and quickly splashes and sinks. It's the choice I make.

*"The harder the conflict, the more glorious the triumph.
What we obtain too cheap, we esteem too lightly; it is dearness
only that gives everything its value. I love the man that can
smile in trouble, that can gather strength from distress and
grow brave by reflection. 'Tis the business of little minds to
shrink; but he whose heart is firm, and whose conscience
approves his conduct, will pursue his principles unto death."*
~ Thomas Paine

Chapter 13 - First Steps, Next Steps, New Steps

"O Lord, teach my heart where and how to seek you, where and how to find you. You are my God, you are my all and yet I've never seen you. You made me and you've remade me, you've bestowed on me every good thing I possess and still I do not know you and have yet to do that for which you made me. Teach me to seek you, Lord, for I cannot seek you unless you teach me or find you unless you show yourself to me. Let me seek you in my desire and let me desire you in my seeking. Let me find you by loving you and let me love you when I find you." Amen.
---from St. Anselm 1033-1109[14]

Batter Up: Post Game Wrap Up (cont'd)

By this time, I think you know where I am coming from. As ominous as it may seem, *face any challenge head on*. New career? Sure. New place and home? Been there, done that. Old friends but not true ones? Ditto. Learning to try to actually walk again? Ok, new steps it was.

By now, I looked forward to therapy because not only am I continually challenging myself, literally during every new step, but I also meet my human need for social interaction. Learning to roll with the punches has become second nature to me.

One month to the day after my massive Pontine stroke, I found myself up on two feet. Barely, mind you, but we all must start somewhere! "Calendar event!" my sister yelled when she came into the room! Both my daily mantra and milestones have been duly noted so I can one day look back and see just how far I've come! Listen, when people are overcome watching you move just one finger, this step is indeed a "big deal".

Learning to walk was originally exhausting. I thought I was climbing Mount Olympus! The bathroom was my next big goal. Looking longingly at a toilet because you drank too much, seems like a lifetime ago. Now, looking longingly at a raised toilet seat, I vowed I'd get there. Milestones were now major motivational factors. So major in fact, I kept (and still do) a record of my achievements, with countless firsts still to look forward to. Figuring out both next and/or new steps was and still is both exciting and a bit daunting.

Since this was all I was able to control, I used several types of mind games to keep my cognitive abilities agile. I named everything: human and otherwise! If it helped me reach a goal or kept me comfortable, it had a name. Thus, I made it my daily goal to learn the name of every doctor, nurse, aide or therapist who helped me. I asked them to write their names on the whiteboard near me, and I devised a system to link names with faces.

The simple naming of objects included:

- Walter the Wheelchair
- Freddie the Hoyer lift
- Cathy the Catheter (you already met her)
- Tommy the Toilet

Still, while my newfound object friends were helpful in their own time and place, I wished them well and hoped the door didn't hit them in the proverbial butt as they left one by one. Meanwhile, less assistance and more milestones began filling my calendar. Even the nursing aides and therapists got into the act, wanting to note various achievements.

All wasn't a barrel of laughs, however. One day my PCP came to visit. I woke from a nap with an excruciating pain shooting through my left arm where the pic-line had been inserted. I cried out in pain, "Jim, help me!" Without a word, he took off like a shot to locate Dr. V (I don't believe I ever saw anyone move so fast!).

Dr. V. removed the pic-line in less than a minute. Unfortunately, it had become infected and the pain was relentless, so much so that my sister insisted on staying overnight and ended up sleeping in a chair in my room. When I awoke around 4 a.m., the pain had not subsided so Patty had the doctor on-call come in. They decided I need to go back to the emergency room at Lahey.

Did you know that each day a person is immobile in bed without movement equates to three days without therapy? Boy, I learned that the hard way. One can slide back to one's former state very quickly. I wanted to get back into my regimen as fast as I could.

When I started to walk, it was such a struggle. I joke a lot, but that never means I take the situation lightly. Grasping at the hospital atrium railing for support, my therapist kept reminding me that I need to learn to use the walker, saying, "You can't take that with you." So little by little I retrained my brain to use the walker for support, and

I upped my goal. If the therapist wanted me to try 10 steps that morning, I'd do 12 and so on.

After a few weeks of 10 foot walks, I was finally able to walk with the assistance of a leg brace and walker. That was huge, and I broke down crying. I made it! I can do this I'm now walking about 150 feet in a given day which doesn't seem like much, but I eventually want to get my driver's license back after I've modified my car to the necessary specifications. What a milestone that will be!

I was now ready to move to another step-down residential facility on my journey homeward. One would think I was looking forward to the change because that would move me a step closer to home.

Transitions

Transition day arrived, another step closer to home, which filled me with conflicting emotions. I need to calm my nerves for the 4.3-mile journey just down the road. Smiling as I am squeezed into a child-sized transport wheelchair (seriously), I bid my trusted life savers goodbye and headed towards the unknown.

I arrived to a room which has recently been converted from a 3-person room to a 1-person room that was huge! I was exhausted both mentally and physically from the journey. Tomorrow I'll be excited about the new challenges ahead. Right now, all I want is to sleep, but people are coming in and out of the room. A kind nurse comes in and conducts a thorough evaluation/exam. I'm treated again to answering tons of questions. What a revolving door!

Finally, I say to myself, I'll get the nap I so desperately need. The nurse transfers me over to the bed which someone has forgotten to set the lock on, and we both fell in a heap onto the bed. Nice to meet you, sir, I might add. This does not bode well for first impressions. You have to really learn to roll with those punches, and tumbles! On the bright side, we both have fallen onto the bed, not the floor.

Still, I cried myself to sleep that night, overwhelmed by so much change and trauma. Can you blame me? Give yourself a break too!

There were a few more punches. I was working one day on a machine with the Occupational Therapist. The machine for my arms sat on top of a hospital table. It fell straight down, ripping out the feeding tube that had been surgically input into my stomach. I thought the OT was going to pass out when she saw the blood and tube on my lap. The nurses ran in to control the bleeding.

Just as they finished, my sister called. She spoke to the head nurse, who tried in vain to reassure her that I was ok. My sister Patty told me she'd call back in five minutes. When those five minutes came and went, I knew I'd see her in 25 minutes. Like clockwork, she appeared at my door and stayed until the entire situation was resolved to her satisfaction. God bless her.

Another time, I was trying to learn how to walk with a cane, and the PT became distracted, just at the moment I fell, hitting my head on the linoleum floor. This resulted in a very nice goose egg on my head --- and another trip to the ER, due to the reason for my stroke in the first place.

<u>Lesson Learned:</u>
You really have to take these situations thrown at you in stride. Wear them even as a badge of honor. Not doing so will allow them to consume and overwhelm you.

Broken Wings

Ever challenging myself, has been my motus operandi. There are always instances one step forward, two steps back situations in life. One such instance happened 5 years after my stroke.

While exercising with my PCA, I attempted to get up from an old chair provided by the building where I reside. While the building is supposed to accommodate the handicapped and elderly, their furniture is 40 years old and does not even remotely come close to accommodating the building inhabitants. Guidelines and laws from ADA and FHA go.

Exercising and learning to sit in various chairs has been a constant challenge. As I was attempted to rise from the very low chair, I fell straight down breaking both legs!

I ended up bedridden in the hospital and rehab for 6+ weeks. Gone were some achievements I previously made. It took my over 5 months to regain them all.

Silver Linings occur whenever and wherever if you open yourself up to them. One huge silver lining for me began after I broke both of my legs. Ever since the stroke I was not able to move ant part of my left foot due to the stroke 5 years earlier. Once I began receiving home physical therapy, the therapist and aid began really stretching the left foot. The aid even began scratching it as if one would a dog's stomach.

This action began to reactivate some of the dormant muscles in the foot. I have begun to have movement in my foot and toes. I blessing deriving from an unfortunate event indeed!

If you are like me, a child of the 70s and 80s, a popular song comes to mind. can you guess what it may be?

If you guessed Broken Wings by Mister, Mister, then you get an Attaboy! Don't laugh but Mister Mister's one hit wonder refrain really resonates with me here. The lyrics are as follows.

Broken Wings

Refrain
Take these broken wings
And learn to fly again
And learn to live so free
And when we hear the voices sing
The book of love will open up
And let us in

Now I'm not suggesting here that you break your legs foot in order to find your silver lining. Instead, just allow yourself to be open and welcoming to the gift should it arise.

Think About It
Have you had a Silver Lining event or moment?

THE YOUTH OF AMERICA SINGERS   1982 European Concert Tour

Chapter 14- Giving Back To Society

"I am like a bird singing in the thicket of thorns."
---St. Francis de Sales

Batter Up: Forced Early Retirement

Meet adversity head on and channel its results into a positive experience!

After the stroke, I was in a quandary as to how to contribute to society. My singing voice was gone. Now, so too was my ability to care for myself independently and to earn a living wage. Gone in a flash was the high-paying and responsible job which I thoroughly enjoyed, replaced by my wheelchair, walker and leg brace (without the latter, I am literally bed-ridden). While still in the rehab facility, my first priority was to figure out just how I could return home. I need some "adaptations" to my residence, or it couldn't happen.

Remember that "Extreme Home Makeover" show that remodeled homes for a worthy family? I thought of taking that concept on a smaller scale as I reached out to the local community that I'd been actively involved in for help. My cousin Donna wrote a beautiful letter that was posted to social media (thank God for Facebook!) and the response was wonderful! Never dismiss or minimize the important role social media can play in both a positive or negative way.)

Once people heard of my plight, many banded together to assist me in making my dream a reality. Steve McKenna, a local Greater Boston realtor I knew, contacted Martin Conneely of Conneely Contracting Inc., a local contractor. Together they donated their expertise, time and money to remodel my stairs and bathroom to become handicapped-accessible. Overwhelming was indeed an understatement!

It didn't stop there. Friends organized a Help Regina Day and 20 people came, including a few I hadn't seen since high school 30 years before. We all enjoyed a day of fun, laughs and fellowship as they focused on rearranging my furniture and cleaning. They became once again dear friends who I see often to socialize with today. A local moving company sent over a few men to rearrange my bedroom, which was wonderful since I had been sleeping on the daybed until this event occurred! A family member even donated thousands of dollars to pay for a chairlift so I could get up and down the flight of stairs safely.

Events such as these reveal the true character of an individual. One of my dear friends donated money, allowing me to get special chairs and to help acquire a service dog, which I'm still raising money for. (Did you know that it costs anywhere between $15,000 and $20,000 to professionally raise and train a certified handicapped assistance dog?)

What can I do in my own way to give back to society? If I'm not in therapy, I volunteer my services to the local rehabilitation hospital in which I was a patient I was asked to become the co-chair of the Patient and Family Advocacy Committee (PFAC), which addresses patients' medical needs from a patients' perspective. The committee has instituted some wonderful programs that have been implemented as a result of the group being always committed to continual improvement in quality. It is a wonderful opportunity to get collaborative insights from senior staff, nurses, OTs, PTs and patients alike. Below is a wonderful example of a PFAC mission and vision statement such as the one used for Valley Health System in New Jersey.

- http://www.valleyhealth.com/FastFacts.aspx?id=5552

[15]Another rewarding endeavor is to share my story with regional and national faith-based groups as well as the medical professional community at large. My 12-year struggle has been turned into a rewarding encounter of meeting wonderful, kind souls. These people are on their own journey, engaged in growing in both faith and professional practice. Many of these devoted people (doctors, nurses, personal care attendants, occupational and physical therapists) are living witnesses who dedicate their lives to serving humanity.

I look forward to working on redefining how I too can give back to humanity finding my new voice and reality. My own desire is to volunteer my time, utilizing both my faith and professional expertise to help enlighten and engage both myself and other individuals through open dialogue. Everyone has a story to tell. We need to be open, to listen.

Meeting adversity head on can change "negative" results into positive experiences.

*"It does not matter how slowly you go
so long as you do not stop."*
~ Confucius

Think About It
Have you met someone who's life has been changed?
If so, how did it change yours?
What's been your new beginnings moment?
How are you acting this out in your everyday life?

Chapter 15 – Tips, Tricks and Terms

Ok, so you jumped directly to this chapter and the next, you cheated. Don't worry --- I forgive you. But once you're done digesting these recommendations, may I suggest that you return to Chapter 1. You won't be disappointed.

Issue	Recommendation
Acupuncture	Some insurances do cover it but only on a-case by-case basis for certain illnesses or pain management associated with it. Ask your insurance company to possibly allow a certified and licensed doctor in acupuncture to perform the treatment. Ask them for the opportunity for the review board to specifically review your case prior to doling out the $100-plus out of pocket.
ADL	**A**ssistance of **D**aily **L**iving – both equipment aids and service provided by people to assist you in dressing, household chores, showers, etc.
As Caregivers, Take Time For Yourself!	You're going through a traumatic experience as well. Cut yourself some slack here!
DME	**D**urable **M**edical **E**quipment for functional use. May or may not be covered under insurance. Check with your insurance carrier.

Don't Judge Your Recovery By Others	Everyone is unique. What might be their challenge might not be yours, and vice versa. Avoiding comparisons saves frustration!
Family Support	Integral to a successful outcome, whether the family is biological or a network of friends.
Give Feedback	No matter how large or small. They can't help you if they don't get it! Or even learn to better their current policies, practices or procedures.
Helping Hands	People really want to help! They won't know what you need until asked! They're not mind-readers.
Humor (HUGS)	Humor is a critical emotion in one's recovery! As Julia Fox Garrison states in her book, "Don't Leave Me This Way...or you'll be sorry when I get up!", **Humor Ultimately Gives Strength**
Injuries	You're not immune. Expect the unexpected.
Learn Who's Who!	Take the time and learn caregivers' names. Hospitals normally have white boards. Make sure they update it for every shift. Doctors, nurses, CNAs (certified nursing assistants), therapists, other hospital staff integral to the success of your care. Greet them by their name when they enter or leave your room. This will help your cognitive training and so your caregivers you recognize that they are on team YOU!
LTD	Long Term Disability Insurance. Most companies offer that as a benefit. If they do so, take it! It may cost you extra and you may never need it. But by doing so, you will be ready to tackle the unexpected.
Never Be Embarrassed Or Modest	Listen if the caregiver wants to help. If they don't have one of their own, more than likely they've seen one. Get over yourself; 50% of the population is physically made in your image.

PT1	Forms that Medicare (or for Patients in MA-MassHealth). Help with free transportation to doctor and health facilities. Your PCP needs to complete and submit the information. If approved, you'll get assistance. See if a similar service is offered in you area.
Roll With The Punches	Self-explanatory. It will make your life more tolerable.
Speak Up For Yourself!	In all instances. Recall the old adage:"You are your best advocate." If you can't do it yourself, get a trusted member of your family or friend and be sure to document your wishes BEFOREHAND!

Chapter 16 - Final Thoughts

"To be grateful is to recognize the Love of God in everything He has given us - and He has given us everything. Every breath we draw is a gift of His love, every moment of existence is a grace, for it brings with it immense graces from Him. Gratitude therefore takes nothing for granted, is never unresponsive, is constantly awakening to new wonder and to praise of the goodness of God. For the grateful person knows that God is good, not by hearsay but by experience. And that is what makes all the difference."
- Thomas Merton[16]

From a practical perspective, the most thoughtful lesson learned I can impart, other than believing in yourself, is the practical advice for every person to acquire Long Term Disability (LTD) if offered from your place of employment! Had I not done so, I would have gone from receiving an upper middle class career and comfortable salary to living entirely on Social Security Disability Insurance (SSDI) at least for a set period of time. This 40% LTD of your salary, will in fact, help supplement your SSDI. I wasn't even 50 years old when my debilitating stroke occurred after both a freak accident and subsequent miss-medical diagnosis.

From a spiritual perspective, I could have written a 200+ page book focusing on just one illness, never mind multiple books on my medical illnesses and challenges, or simply the faith-based aspect of my life, but that would deny the essence of who I am and the importance of both aspects in my journey.

If you feel you were hit over the head with repeated references to God in this book, you were. You see, God's in charge here, not you or me. We're here either to learn something about ourselves, or to be a vessel through which we can touch others' lives, and to show and share God's unwavering love for each and every one of God's creations.

The human body and mind forever seek purpose and meaning. Whatever trials, tribulations, or triumphs we experience are but momentary glimpses of what we humans can accomplish when we open up our minds and hearts (especially in silence) to listen to God speak to us of our own purpose in this life. By releasing ourselves of our own mental and physical limitations, we can truly witness the beauty of all of God's living and loving creations.

John Michael Talbot, in his insightful book *The Jesus Prayer*[17] (which I highly recommend), gives what I consider to be a wonderful analogy of my health challenges and rewards. In Talbot's book, he explains that bread undergoes extreme transformations in its process, changing from one form to another; being broken down to rise yet again anew.

This intricate process involves the following eight-steps:
1. Harvesting Wheat
2. Threshing
3. Winnowing
4. Ground Into Flour
5. Making the Dough
6. Rising In The Pan
7. The Oven
8. Cooling

Music, as well, allows us to pray more wholly with God. The music which soothes this savage heart includes compositions so beautifully written by Talbot, Fr. Liam Lawton, Christopher Walker, Fr. Jan Michael Joncas, David Haas, Rory Cooney and Tony Alonso to name a few. Their songs, reflecting a wide array of composition styles. They challenge each of us to stop for even a few moments in our busy lives to focus again on our faith journey. Only then can we build a deeper relationship with the Creator.

My fervent hope and prayer is that each of you be open to God as you encounter the Divine Creator when the Spirit attempts to speak to you during your life's journey.

"God knows our situation; He will not judge us as if we had no difficulties to overcome. What matters is the sincerity and perseverance of our will to overcome them."
*~ **CS Lewis.***

Chapter 17 - Resource Recommendations

This is just a partial list *(in alphabetical order)* of resources. Create your own list and keep in a handy reference binder for easy access.

Who They Are	What They Do	Website
Advantage Medical	Equipment, supplies for disabilities	www.advantagemedical.com 800.577.5694
American Institute of Stress	Relating to cardiovascular, gastrointestinal and diseases of the skin	www.strokeassociation.org 888.478.7653
Easter Seals	Service to individuals with disabilities and special needs	www.easterseals.com 800.221.6827
Institute for Patient, Family-Centered Care	Promoting collaborative, empowering relationships among patients, families, and health-care professionals	www.ipfcc.org 301-652-0281

Lancet	Medical information resource of various topics. For professionals. Also a good resource for patients. European site	www.thelancet.com
Merck Medical	Healthcare professional Resource Standard for over 100 years. Home Edition now available in paperback, hardcover and online. Excellent resource	ww.merck.com
National Institute of Neurological Disorders and Stroke	For both the public and private sectors, information, articles, studies training and research resource	www.ninds.nih.gov 800.352.9424
National Rehabilitation Information Center	Information regarding disabilities, rehabilitation, facilities, support groups.	www.naric.com 800.346.2742
National Stroke Association	Prevention, treatment, rehabilitation, research, support for stroke related issues for patients and families	www.stroke.org 800.787.6537

Neurology Now	Publication provided by American Academy of Neurology and American Brain Foundation	www.aan.com 800.879.1900
Patterson Medical	Equipment, supplies for disabilities (used by therapists)	www.pattersonmedical.com 800.323.5547
Stanford Stroke Center	Informative regarding therapies and clinical trial. Published new developmental findings	www.stanford.edu 800.800.1551

ABOUT THE AUTHOR-HIGHLIGHTS

Regina M Pontes, MBA

- Colleges attended:
    - Mount St. Mary's College, Los Angeles, CA
    - New York Institute of Technology, NYC, NY
    - Harvard University Extension, Cambridge MA
- Publisher of:
    - Songs of the Wilderness
    - I Remember Knowing – Volumes 1 through 6
- Co-chair of PFAC at New England Rehabilitation Hospital, Woburn, MA
- IPFCC member
- Motivational speaker
- Born and raised in Massachusetts.
- Performed on liturgical CDs by Christopher Walker and St. Thomas More Group
- Cantor and soloist for regional and national diocesan events located in Boston, MA and Los Angeles, CA

- Former Quality Manager in R&D and DoD companies. Secret clearance.
- Humanitarian works including
  - Worked with Senator Byron Dorgan's office to secure the removal of a female refugee from war-torn Bosnia. Full college and housing obtained
  - Co-chair Organization of relief concert for hurricanes Katrina and Rita
- Mentor, coach and friend

End Notes

1 © Hallmark card (I received over 100 cards after the stroke! This one nailed it!)

2 © Estate of Walter Anderson

3 © Christopher Walker, internationally acclaimed composer, lecturer, author

4 © Estate of Richard James Michael Pontes *To see more of his works, visit https://www.facebook.com/PoetsCornerRichardsOriginals*

5 Lahey Clinic – healthcare facility – www.lahey.org

6 1980s - One of the original supermodels

7 © Kristin Chenowech CD entitled As I Am. Song entitled Borrowed Angels

8 © David Haas, internationally acclaimed composer, lecturer, author

9 © Charles Strouse - We Love You Conrad from the musical Bye Bye Birdie

10 Keenan Sahin, President and founder of TIAX LLC

11 © Fr. Jan Michael Jonas, internationally acclaimed composer, lecturer, author

12 © Isabella R. Moyer-Author, catholic dialogue, 2011. www.catholicdialogue.com

13 © Lois McMaster Bujold-Author, *The Curse of Chalion*

14 © St. Anselm Quote w/Picture compliments of Fr. Austin Fleming. Visit his blog at http://concordpastor.blogspot.com/

15 Institute for Patient and Family Centered Care – www.ipfcc.org

16 © Thomas Merton, theologian, scholar

17 The Jesus Prayer book by John Michael Talbot

Would you love to share your story?
We'd love to hear it!
Email us today at:
yourpikstory@gmail.com

Printed in the United States
By Bookmasters